Heart Shadows

Carly Dodd

BookLeaf Publishing

India | USA | UK

Presentation by *BookLeaf Publishing*

Web: www.bookleafpub.com

E-mail: info@bookleafpub.com

ISBN: 9789357446730

First edition 2022

& my favourite days were

all the ones

with you in them

—

1

in this life
there have only ever been two things
I am certain of.
one is me,
the other is you.

—

2

and from within
the tiniest flutter,
a wing beat
against my chest
that rippled
the softest,
indiscernible wave
through my veins
my nerves
my fingertips,
and made its way to you

—

3

there is a pull
that draws me to you.
magnetism
or a death wish,
I know not which

—

4

colour in
the spaces of me
I didn't know were blank
fill the parts left empty,
that only you
with your many changing hues
would dare to paint

you threw me up to the sky,
I panicked at the freedom
grand gesture;
crumpled inward,
only to plummet
hard
at your feet.

—

spaces
between fingers between bodies
between hands
growing greater with time
they spread, engulf, swallow you
whole
until there is no out, only in side.
the spaces between will pull you
apart
wrenching   your ventricles
lungs
cells
Stretching, straining
spaces   create spaces
as   the spaces are seen
push each other out, help each other
grow
until   all is space
caught in b e t w e e n.

—

and you were a dream
I could never quite catch
a wave on the shore
I could never pin down,
hold.
to keep you was impossible
but maybe,
if I waited long enough
you just might
wash my way again

−

you speak to me in steps
all you say sticking and punctuating
I hang on to every word,
a tiny foothold
to which I cling
desperately,
shakily
and I know it is only upon these words
that I can climb
and that I shall soon be abandoned
when you stop uttering them;
when I will be left gripping
suspended
until my arms go weak and my legs
give out
and I cannot hold to those words,
grown old and worn with time

—

there is a sadness deep within
that plucks at heart strings
that melancholy harp
which echoes on
in slow refrains
an endless, tragic din

—

this gaping hole
has never left
because you left
too soon

—

like snow that falls gently
floating its way down,
loneliness settled upon me gradually
built up calmly and quietly
until the sheer weight
of it was indisputable
undeniable
and constantly at risk of crushing me
should I dare to move

—

not only did I lose you,
but I lost the me
I was in your eyes

—

memories
once shared,
now mine alone
to have
to hold
and pull out on rainy days

tiny glimmers in the dark

—

you stopped yourself in time
forever young
and wild
and full of a desperate need
to break it all.

shaking your fist at the world
the storms within

that raged inside
and swallowed you whole

—

the lives I might have lived
if I had lived
haunt me.
the things I might have done
if I'd have stayed

to walk this Earth
another day,
to speak my voice
to hear me say:

I love you

one more time

—

when does love end?
how does it fade?
ticks itself away
when does it leave?
dissipate
unclench its mighty fist

love lingers on

clings
warps its fingers around your ribs
and holds
and holds
and never truly lets go

—

17

I thought you'd cut that invisible string
that tied our hearts together,
but you'd only buried it
out of sight
but not so deep that it couldn't be
unearthed
with eager hands
and dirty fingers,
untangling your way
back to me

—

we came to each other broken
both of us in pieces
we fitted one another together
with messy tape and clumsy glue
put back the parts of us
torn apart
by callous love
and selfish needs.
we poured our love into the cracks
sealed them shut with
kisses
and kindness
slowly mending
and when we began
to look whole again
it was impossible
not to see
each other's fingerprints
smeared all over
one another's hearts

—

lay with me
and tell me all the ways
we are
and aren't,
or maybe could be.

the things we never were,
never are
never can see

but dream of all the same

—

wrap me in your colours
cover me with light
hide me in your shadows
fill me with your fight
I want to be
what you are
I want to be

—

fold me in your starlight
always let me in
dress me in your whispers
shroud me in your skin
bury me in words
share your secret sin

I want to be
forever within